MAGIC RABBIT (LLI PIKA) COLORING BOOK

CRYSTAL
COLORING BOOKS

ISBN-13: 978-1717129161
ISBN-10: 1717129161

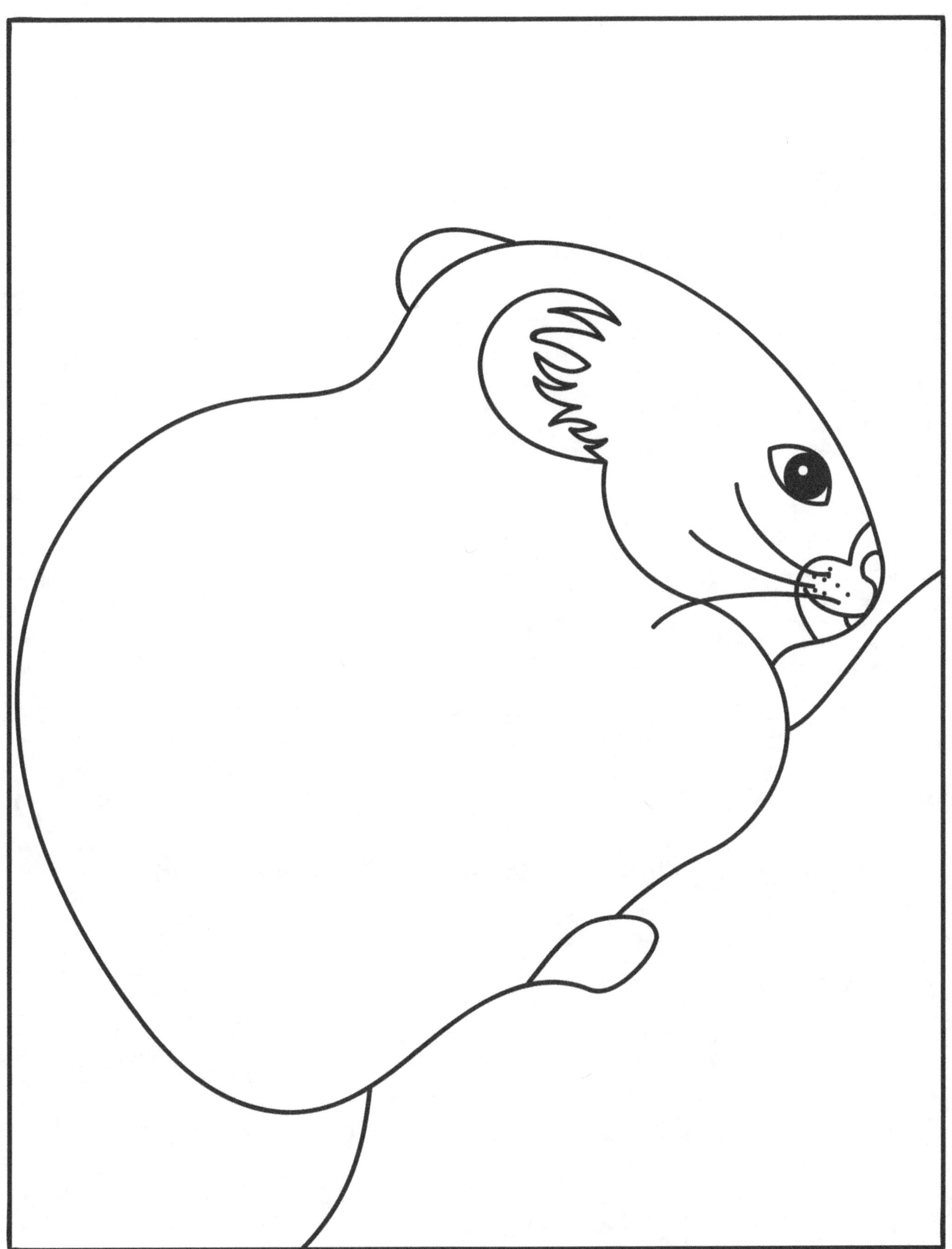

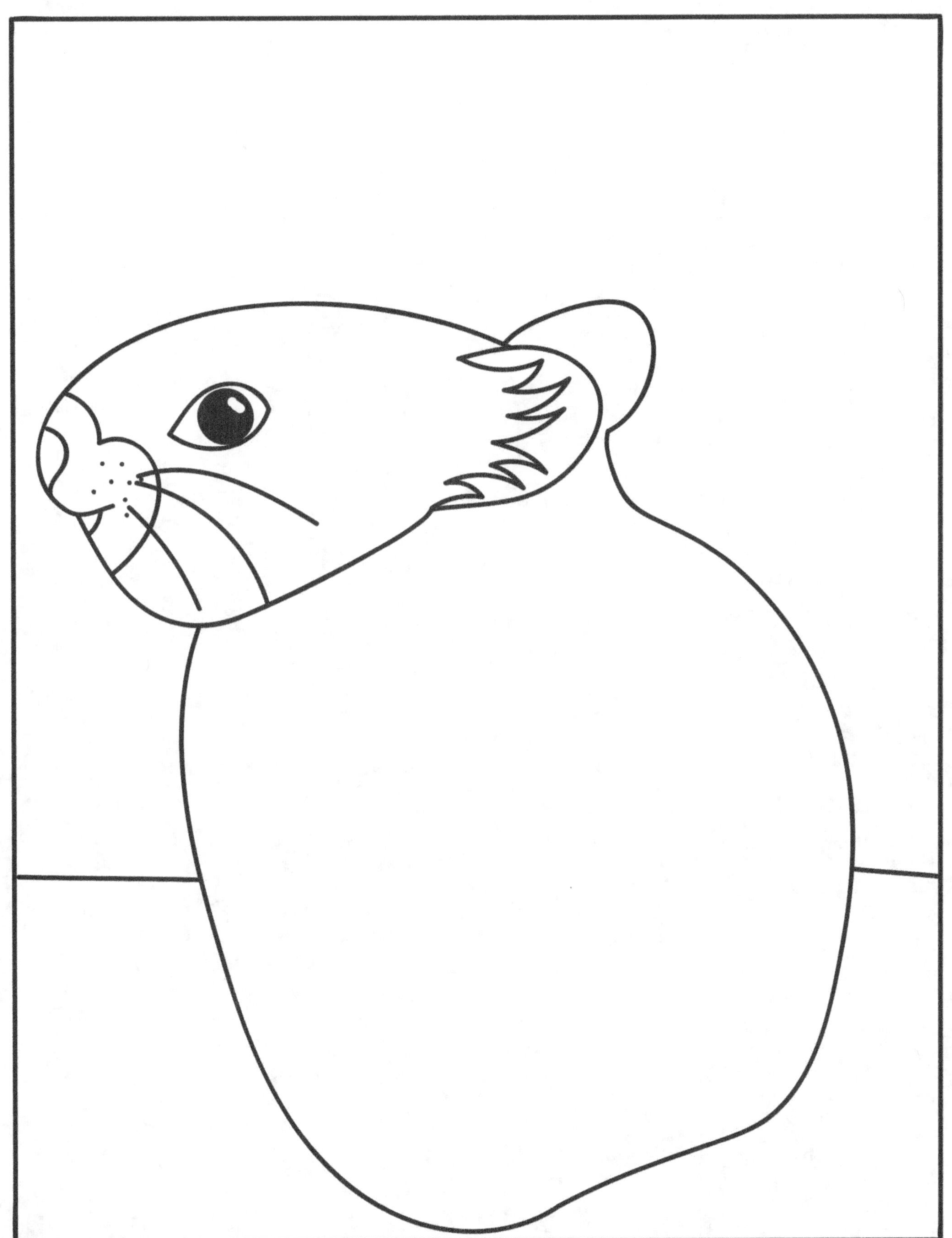

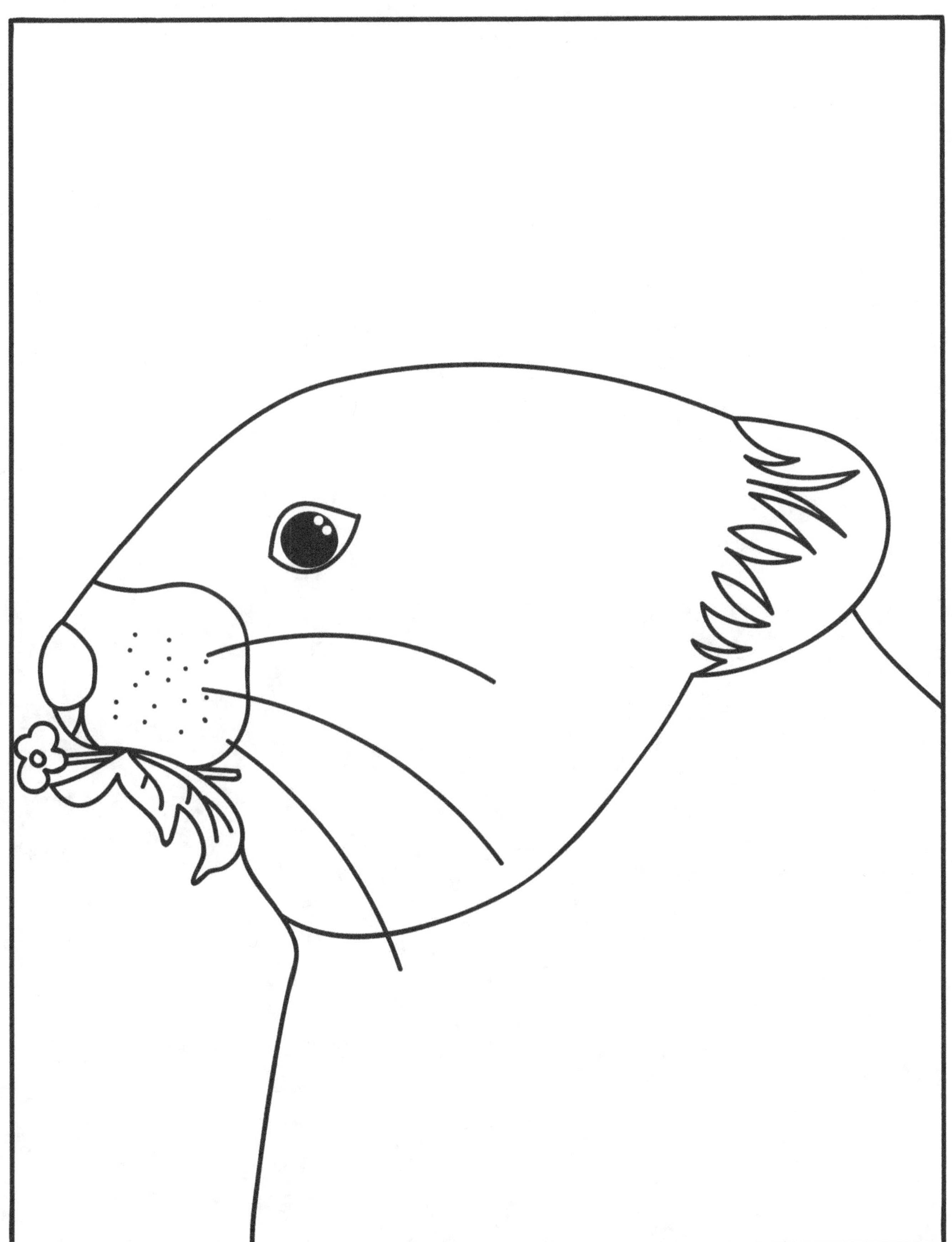

COLOR TEST PAGE

COLOR TEST PAGE

www.ingramcontent.com/pod-product-compliance
Lightning Source LLC
Chambersburg PA
CBHW080238260726
48658CB00008B/3152